CHOICES

CHOICES

Like waves going to distant shores, will we ever really understand the consequences of our choices?

SYLVIA RAMOS PANEQUE

ARPress
ILLUMINATING IDEAS,
EMPOWERING VOICES

ARPress
45 Dan Road Suite 5
Canton MA 02021

Hotline: 1(888) 821-0229
Fax: 1(508) 545-7580

Ordering Information:

Quantity sales. Special discounts are available on quantity purchases by corporations, associations, and others. For details, contact the publisher at the address above.

Printed in the United States of America.

ISBN-13:   Paperback   979-8-89330-459-6
              eBook   979-8-89330-460-2

Library of Congress Control Number: 2024900750

Table of Contents

DEDICATION

I dedicate this book to the Trinity. Father God sent his only Son, Jesus, to die for all of us and pay a price we could never pay! Jesus sat down at the Father's right hand and then sent the Holy Spirit to be our best friend and lead us into all Truth! Holy Spirit moves upon our hearts and reveals to us all the wonders of Heaven and gives strength and wisdom to face each new day if we let Him. The best thing I ever did was humble myself and cry out, "forgive me and lead me into all you have created me to be!"

Thank you for saving me from me. I am looking forward to eternity with all my forever family!

CHAPTER ONE
EYES WIDE OPEN

Mexico City, January 21, 1981

It was 5:00 a.m. when we landed in Mexico City. My sister, Pam, and I arrived from Lima, Peru. I was mentally and physically exhausted. I could not rest on the flight and kept going over everything I had just experienced. Getting through the airport in Lima was a wake-up call, to say the least. The security at the airport was military with machine guns! I was praying, "God, please let me get out of Peru." I sensed the darkness all around that airport. Then, finally, the reality sank in: life would be unthinkable if we got caught here with the cocaine. Talk about being in a bubble! I wished I had put on my thinking cap long before this.

What a stark contrast to a few days earlier in Machu Picchu. The people, the food, and the epic scenery of Machu Picchu made it an amazing place. Now, here I was, praying I could get out of Peru. Our cab driver had a cross hanging from his mirror but as we made small talk, the cross broke and fell to the floor. It was a sign, and as we passed a building that looked like a courthouse, I was feeling a bit queasy.

I was asking myself what made me think this was a good idea? Oh, that's right, they would pay for the trip and give me one thousand dollars in cash! Drugs. I did not think they were a big deal. In my world, most of the people I knew did some self-medicating. Though, I didn't care for drugs because I did not like the feeling of being out of control, seemed funny now, right? So I understood why many people felt they needed them to take a break from reality.

My break was travel. I lived in Hawaii and worked in Japan and Kyoto as a D.J. I loved coming into contact with the different cultures and people.

Also, I was comfortable in countries that didn't speak English, so I was not bothered when I was clueless about what they were saying. I guess I was clueless about many things, though, and I was in my little world.

Just before leaving Peru, I got violently ill, probably from letting a marmoset monkey, the smallest in the world and so cute, give me a grape to eat. Imagine the bacteria from the hand of that little creature? Otherwise, we would have been on our way to Rio de Janeiro for Carnival, a festival that happens once a year in Brazil. If we got caught with drugs in Rio, it would have been much worse. The sentence would be very long, and we could have been sentenced to life and never get out!

After getting off the plane, Pam and I went to different lines. While waiting for quite a while, I noticed my sister walking past me, and I said, "What about these lines?" She rolled her eyes and didn't say a word, so I assumed she was going to the lady's room. It was then I noticed someone was walking behind her. He took her away to the back somewhere. From a distance, I could hear someone yelling something in Spanish.

The man in front of me looked like he might have been an American businessman. He must have understood every word they were yelling because his eyes were as big as saucers when he turned around and stared at me in shock. Then he backed away from me with a look that said, "She is not with me!"

Someone came up from behind, grabbed me, and led me back to where my sister was.

Entering the room, I heard my sister swearing at the officers. She was furious, and I thought they understood every word she was saying, and since were not in America—that was not a good idea!

The officers asked me if I had anything. I lifted my pant legs and gave them the two packages of cocaine. I couldn't hide it now and these people were doing their job. I was in the wrong, not them!

A federale took me to a small room next to where they had my sister. The federale looked at me with compassion, and I could only imagine what he was thinking. Then, suddenly, the door opened, and I saw my sister. She was still swearing at them, and she was handcuffed. They were spinning her around and he had a rag wrapped around her head. They were hitting her with something—a cloth with something inside it, and someone had unzipped her pants, wanting to scare her, I imagine?

My heart sank. I said a quick prayer. "Please, God, don't let them hurt my sister!" I looked at the officer with tears in my eyes and I said, "Please, please, help my sister." I believe the officer had mercy on me because he left the room and soon returned with my sister.

An overwhelming sick feeling engulfed me. I could not imagine how the ripples of this event would change everything in my world, but I knew I was trapped and I was not getting out of this one.

The federale's loaded us into an unmarked car with lights. I was in the front seat with the kind officer, and Pam was in the back seat with another officer.

The traffic in Mexico City was crazy. There was so much traffic, and everyone was going in different directions. It was so bad the officer was driving on the sidewalks to get around it.

When we finally arrived at the building where the agents worked at, they put us in an elevator and took us up very high into the building, to maybe the eighth floor. Then, one of the federale's placed us in a small room and left.

I said, "We need to make sure that we have our story straight, say it was all my idea." It was not. My sister's boyfriend, Manfred, approached me with the idea, but I agreed to do it. And since I am the older sister, so it was all on me. "Tell them I told you we were going to buy alpaca rugs."

Looking back, they probably could hear everything I was saying. Anyway, we stuck to the story.

I imagined they knew we wouldn't be hungry because they never offered us anything, not even water. So much for human rights. Although, when in a situation like ours, that was the least of our problems. Hunger and thirst were the last things on our minds.

They placed us in a large, empty room with a window on the inside but with no outside window. I was thankful that we had bought warm jackets in Cusco because we used them as pillows; the floor was very uncomfortable. There was no table, chair, or anything in the room but us.

An officer was outside the room, and he put a long table in front of the window. He had a machine gun, possibly an AK47, and slept on that table all night. I guess it was just in case the Sinaloa Cartel tried to break us out. Not a chance, though. The cartel didn't know us. We were tiny fish in a huge pond!

The only ones wondering about us would have been our boyfriends, as they were the only ones who knew we were on our way home. But since we never called once we arrived in Mexico City, I was sure they knew something wasn't right.

The following morning the federale's took us to a vast room with only two chairs in the middle. Federale agents were lining all four walls. They stood us on those chairs, rolled up our pant legs, and stuffed our boots with the cocaine. They took pictures—many, many pictures. As they spoke in Spanish, I only imagined what they were saying: "typical mules." I sometimes wonder what they did with those pictures and only God knows what happened with the cocaine.

After we left the building, they took us to a small jail on the outskirts of town. Now, this was a special place: It was all concrete, no toilet paper, no mattress, no blankets, and no heat. Just the two of us, as far as I could tell, in this small jail. You might think Mexico City doesn't need heated buildings. Well, Mexico City's elevation is 7,382 feet, and it did get cold. But, of course, it was also, January. Again, I was thankful for those jackets.

We had been there for several hours when one of the guards finally brought us something on a paper plate, maybe refried beans and corn tortillas. We were not hungry, so we just took a few bites and set the paper plates aside. We both laid down on the same concrete slab, and Pam quickly dozed off.

As I was resting, I repeatedly thought about how my children and family would be affected. All of a sudden, I could hear movement coming down the hall. I thought it might be a rodent from the sound of it.

I was on the inside of the concrete slab and the sound was getting closer. I saw a rat standing up on its hind legs as I looked over. Pam woke up and saw the rat five inches from her face. It was about the size of a small cat but fatter, looking her right in the eyes! Pam screamed and jumped about six inches in the air, and it scurried away.

She was noticeably shaken and said, "Please, I need to sleep on the inside!" So I took the outside position. I knew the creature had smelled the food we had not eaten, so I took the food and placed it by the cell bars. It returned, took the paper plate, and I did not see it again. I was thankful I had never been afraid of rodents, or I would have been traumatized like my sister.

Later that evening, we heard the voices of two males in a cell. Naturally, we were curious, so we climbed up on the top concrete slab and found our heads could fit through the crossbars. So we started asking our fellow inmates why they were there.

It turned out that they were also caught with drugs and were also Americans. They were transporting marijuana and traveling in a motor home; of course, they would seize all property. I wondered later how things turned out for them.

The following day, we had visitors. The attorneys had heard that two Americans had been arrested and taken into custody at the airport. Knowing we would not get a phone call, they came to find out if they could call someone for us. They knew how to drum up business. I was so thankful. It could have been months before we could make a phone call. We gave them our boyfriends' (Avi and Manfred) numbers in Los Angeles, and I was sure they would be distraught when they found out we would not be coming home.

Pam, Manfred, Avi, and I were all living in L.A. I was working in the wholesale jewelry business with gold and diamonds. Avi was Israeli and had introduced me to some friends of his, and they asked me to work for them. They were a wonderful Israeli couple named Ari and Ora who came to the States with Israel's dance team. With some small change in their pockets, they decided to stay in America. They had come a long way, and I was thankful to be working for them. I was taking my vacation and going to Lima to attend a friend's wedding, or so they thought.

Getting to know the Israelis was very special to me. They showed me how to work hard and that working was not a chore but an opportunity to improve your life. There were no free rides. You had to get busy and do your part.

I would have never considered carrying drugs if I had paid better attention to them. But I had made another wrong choice, like leaving my two children with their father while I tried to see what life was all about. I was the oldest of a large family; my parents were married when they were very young.

They had eight children in ten years. I'll say more about that later.

Upon reflection, there were so many things I could have done differently with my life. But, unfortunately, or fortunately, depending on how you look at it, I had to face the music and take a long hard look at my life. The trip to South America had changed my life forever, no doubt, but I could honestly say it needed changing.

When I was living in L.A., and a few months before I went to Peru, I had this dream about driving very fast on the freeway, and all of a sudden, the traffic was backed-up and stopped. Then, as I was about to crash, I woke up. I was sure that was a warning from God—it was time to wake up, Sylvia! My life in the fast lane was about to end.

For me, the fast lane was get-up-and-go, don't look back, and let someone else take care of your responsibilities. But now that I was forced to stop and look at my life, things were coming into focus.

It took some time to realize I could be a part of the answer, not the problem. I thanked God for His chastening. I was sure it kept me from something far worse.

Proverbs 3:13, New American Standard Bible says, *"Blessed is the person who finds wisdom and obtains understanding!"*

This event was the beginning of wisdom and understanding for me!

Proverbs 22:11 says: *"He (or she) that loves pureness of heart, for the grace of his (or her) lips the King shall be his (or her) friend."*

As I study the Scriptures for wisdom, this one stands out. I believe God is saying that if your motives are pure, and you are seeing the good in others and not looking for faults, wanting to help others, and not looking for a way to take advantage of them. Then, God will lead you into Truth.

CHAPTER TWO

THE BIG HOUSE

Mexico City, January 26, 1981

After a few days in that small jail, they loaded us into the back of a small pickup with a camper on it. It had two long benches, one on each side. The ride was cramped, and the smells of the outskirts of Mexico City were not pleasant; my hunger pains disappeared.

It was funny how when my choices had taken complete control of my life away from me, and my vision for the future was nothing but blackness, hunger seemed to fade into that darkness.

I was clueless about our actual location, and when we arrived at the men's prison in Norte, I was baffled. As they paraded us through the booking quarters, I felt like we were on display for all those souls with peering eyes—eyes that had distant looks in them, looks that said they had no hope. I was sure that most of them grew up in survival mode, got by, and survived; most of the world probably did that. Neither Pam nor I spoke Spanish, so we were confused.

First, they did fingerprints and photos, then they took us to a small room with a window, where you could see a judge on the other side of the glass. A young girl and boy were at his side, maybe six and seven, and the judge was in a wheelchair. It must have been a "bring your kids to work" day!

We had an interpreter letting us know what was being said; we would be looking at seven to fourteen years! That was an eye-opener, so we sank a little deeper into our sorrow. We were there for several hours, and then we were off to the infamous Santa Martha.

We arrived around nine or so in the evening. The heifers (the inmates' name for the guards) proceeded to the top floor and put us in the isolation unit. I thought, *Isolation? Are they keeping us in isolation until they decide if we will fit in with the population?* The cell block had tiny rooms, eight by ten feet, and we were in the last cell on the left.

After settling into our tiny space, we picked which mat (two inches thick and on the floor) we wanted, then went to find the toilets. Once again, big surprise. The bathrooms had toilets overflowing with excrement, about two or three inches above the top. There were several toilets in this section. I guessed they had not turned on the water for weeks. When there was no water, no flushing. So we were standing there staring in shock and thinking, *How are we supposed to do the big job?* There was no toilet paper either; you needed to bring your own. I am sure you can imagine it was not the beautiful smell of gardenias either! Thank God they turned on the water the next day.

Let me tell you how they flushed the toilets in Santa Martha. It helped if you had a bucket of water and a small can to dip into the bucket of water to pour into the toilet. Inmates needed to use it sparingly because they did not turn the water on very often, twice a month if you were lucky.

It was impossible to flush all that stuff down without any water! It was a good thing we had not been eating and didn't need to do a big job. The following day we were awakened by a woman calling us (flojo) lazy, telling us it was time to get up and clean our cell. She gave us a stick, a rag, and no water; we were pushing the dirt around and out of the room.

I noticed a woman coming out of the cell, the cell right across from ours, and she looked me in the eyes. A cold chill went down my spine. She was an older woman with the blackest eyes I had ever seen; there was no life, she was dead inside! I found out months later that she was in for homicide, so the story went; she had done an unspeakable thing to her husband.

Thankfully, we were only isolated for a few weeks until they decided we would fit in, and they put us in the main population. We were happy to be leaving that area but wondered how we would manage when we didn't speak Spanish. How would we communicate?

So many things were running through my mind. Did the attorneys get in touch with the guys? The only way I could keep my sanity was to take it one day at a time. I found that reading was a great escape.

Santa Martha had concrete floors, stairs, and walls, and I guessed that was a good thing since sanitation could be an issue. They had several different cell sizes. The first cell was about ten by twelve feet, a little bigger than the last, and it had a set of bunks on each side of the cell. We were settling in when a woman entered the cell and I could tell she was unhappy about us moving in with her.

Her name was Norma, and she did not speak English, but anger was an international language, and she made our lives miserable. We could feel the tension, which was the last thing we needed.

Norma's looks said it all: "Don't even think about touching anything." The word must have gotten out that we were not welcome in Norma's cell, and the next day they moved us to a new place, which was the last move until we left. Later, we became friends with Norma, so it all worked out in the end.

This last cell was a large one, maybe twelve by twelve feet, with eight bunks, two-inch mattresses, and one blanket with one sheet. The two-inch mat was uncomfortable, but we were in prison, not the Hilton, after all. Also, someone had put a piece of fabric up to cover the toilet area for some privacy. Thank God for small favors.

Our cell was known as the American unit since we were all from the States. Patty was from California, Karen was from Florida, Pam and I were from Seattle originally, and Manuela was born in Cuba.

Manuela's case broke my heart. Manuela and her husband traveled to South America and picked up some cocaine. The first trip went well, and they decided to try it again. Unfortunately, the next time, they were not lucky and were picked up at the airport just like us.

Manuela's husband was American and qualified to go on the prisoner exchange, but Manuela could not. Although she had not applied for her citizenship, she had been in the U.S.

for over twenty years and had three children; one of them was still in high school, and she was seventeen years old. So she was not an American citizen, and Cuba did not have an exchange. Furthermore, I was sure not many people wanted to go to Cuba; Fidel would not have accepted them anyway.

She was devastated, and we helped her as much as possible. She would help us do our laundry with a washboard by hand, cook for us, and clean. We would give her money. Avi and Manfred were sending money to the American Embassy, and it would be put on our books every month.

We had a hot plate that we purchased at the commissary, so Manuela had something to use for cooking. And she was an excellent cook, and I was thankful she was with us!

Our embassy had brought some national geographic magazines, and I had decorated the walls with pictures from the magazines. In addition, we put egg cartons over the vents to cut down the noise from the outside. I was amazed that we could do all that. Maybe it was because we had our embassy behind us?

After getting settled in for about a month, they told us we needed to get a job, and the only thing we could do that didn't require speaking Spanish was to clean the prison. So, there we were again with a stick and a rag. We had a bucket of water this time, though the water was quickly dirty and the only water we would get. It was pointless, but I guessed the prison staff felt it was essential to keep everyone busy.

The problem with me going up and down those concrete stairs all the time was that my knees didn't like it. So, I went off to the infirmary. They took X-rays and confirmed I had a bad knee, so going up and down the concrete stairs would not work for me. But Pam was a different story. Laura, the lead of cleaning, made her miserable. So, Pam spoke with someone in the office and they took her off the cleaning crew. A few months later, Laura would end up in the hole—a place that you never wanted to be. It was a twelve-by-twelve-foot concrete unit, maybe fifty feet from the main building. There was no light and no windows; you slept on the ground and ate food once daily.

She was in the hole for about three weeks, and when she got out, her skin looked gray and sickly; she said she was never going back.

One morning, after being at Santa Martha a few months, an inmate crowded in front of me. I thought it was because I was right near the front of the line. She was about five feet, three inches tall and stout, and she gave me a look that said, "What are you going to do?"

The one good thing about growing up in Rat City (more about that later) was that I knew if I let her push me around, I would live in torment all the time. Since I didn't speak Spanish and she didn't speak English, I grabbed both of her arms, picked her up, and moved her out of the line. She would not be cutting in front of me again. She backed off, and I never had a problem with crowding after that. It took some time, but we purchased a small T.V. from one inmate after receiving our money from the embassy.

I had never had any interest in current events, but now everything about the United States was significant. First, I realized that the hostages in Iran were released while we were apprehended. That cut deep. I imagined how they must have felt, especially since they were innocent, and how terrifying that must have been for them. So many things were happening in the world, and now I was paying attention. I wanted to think about something other than my little messed up world. President Reagan had just taken office. Iran released the American hostages they had been holding. John Hinckley attempted to assassinate President Reagan. And the first space shuttle, Columbia, was launched. However, looking back, I can say having my freedom taken away was necessary to get my attention—not everything was about me, and now I was becoming aware of so many things.

Something happened that probably influenced the rest of our stay, and something exciting came out of that situation. We had been there about three months when Pam and I had started feeling under the weather; trauma could do that to you. I had gone to the infirmary and the nurse told me I needed an injection of some sort and sent me to see the woman responsible for giving it. I thought she didn't like me, or maybe Americans in general, because when she stabbed it in my backside, she made sure she jiggled the needle the whole time and pushed it in very hard, leaving a large bruise.

The next day I decided to tell someone about it. I went to make a complaint, and low and behold, it so happened that whoever oversaw the prisons had sent Antonio LaBastida to see how things were going. Antonio was the nephew of someone in the political arena, and rumors were that things were not going well at the prison. So Antonio was there to investigate. He spoke with me about what had happened and took care of it. We became friends, and I was sure I was allowed many privileges because of our friendship.

Finally, after being there for around three months, we could make a phone call to our families. Of course, I had to stand in line for about two hours as everyone wanted to make a phone call and there was only one phone. I called Monty and Tina (my son and daughter), and my son was so upset. He kept saying, "I want to see you, Mom. Where are you? I am going to run away and come to see you." I kept telling him that was impossible, but he insisted, so I had to tell him I was in prison in Mexico.

It broke my heart having to tell him I was in jail in Mexico, and he could not come and be with me. I knew it would break his heart. How would a young boy cope with that? When Tina found out, her Aunt Phyllis said she found her in the closet sobbing. It broke her little heart. Choices!

Monty and Tina had spent time with Avi and me in Los Angeles weeks before I had left for South America, and we had a wonderful time together. It was hard to send them back, but I knew I had to be strong and established before even thinking about having them with me. At least in Seattle they were with family, and I was sure they were safe. With me being in prison, I knew it would be a long time before I would see them again, let alone have them live with me—a real wake-up call. Time is different when you are in prison; it seems to drag on, and if you let yourself get caught up in self-pity, it will get the best of you.

After four months, I started an exercise class. The prison had a large auditorium that was perfect for the course. Because exercise was an international language, many of the inmates came. They followed the class leader (me) and made the moves. As some of those little ladies tried to lift their legs above their heads, Pam and I laughed so hard.

I guess they had never attempted that kind of move before, and I was not trying to hurt anyone. The class did not last very long because exercise could be like work and most inmates were not interested in any more pain. I realized so many things, how blessed we were in the United States, and my heart went out to so many of those women.

How could we understand the struggles of people who had been through unspeakable things? On May 22, 1981, we had been in prison for four months. I was out in the yard which had many families and children on visitation day, and I walked around the compound.

We came to a little boy; he must have been there to visit his mother. He had something in his little hand and was getting ready to smash it against the wall—it was a kitten! I quickly ran up and grabbed it out of his hand right before he threw it, and I yelled, "No!" He looked at me shocked, started crying, and then ran away. I had no idea how the kitten ended up in the prison courtyard. I just knew it was helpless, and I could not allow it to be hurt.

The kitten was short-haired and a light gray and white. It was very sickly, and I was determined to help, so I took it back to my cell. I did not even consider that I was in prison, and maybe I should have seen if I could even *have* a kitten! The following day when the heifers opened the cell, they saw the kitten lying across my neck and looked shocked. But they said nothing, so I knew I could keep her.

I named her "Little Girl," and she brought much joy and laughter to all of us. I was so thankful that I was allowed to have a kitten. One other positive thing about being locked up was finding a love for reading. Of course, it was an escape and a great one at that. The missionaries came by the prison every month, and I loved seeing them. They were so kind and would bring books. The first book they gave me was *Hinds' Feet on High Places*; it gave me hope and inspiration.

I read *Shogun* in three days, and my eyes were so bloodshot. The way a great writer could capture my imagination was incredible. It took my mind off my here and now.

Pam and I would play cards with a small group of English-speaking inmates, anything to take our minds off the days that could drag on. We had to hide the cards behind the egg carts that covered vents. It was illegal to play cards; maybe they were worried about gambling? We did play with a few pesos, but only pennies worth. I was sure that real gambling could have taken place at Santa Martha, but I knew nothing about it if it did.

After being in Santa Martha for about nine months, we finally went back to court in the men's prison and received a sentence of nine years, which was good because now we could get ready for the prisoner exchange.

Pam and I had been getting ready for the move right after sentencing. I found a Mexican girl, Rosa, who was getting out of prison, and she graciously agreed to take Little Girl, my cat. So, Pam woke up one morning and said, "I had a dream we were leaving today." Sure enough, it happened. We had been there a little over nine months, and on Friday, October 2, 1981, we said "Bye, bye" to Santa Martha prison!

I was sure it would have been very different if Pam and I had not been together.

She would tell me that I should have said nothing when she walked past me in the airport. No way, that was not going to happen. I could not leave my sister; I chose to do it, and we were in it together.

Looking back, we were all in darkness, thinking we were finding a way to get what we wanted by taking a shortcut. But so much of my thinking needed an adjustment, and I had to take a good, hard look at my life… Choices.

PRISONER EXCHANGE

On December 30, 1976, the U.S. signed a treaty with Mexico to exchange prisoners when the awareness of the unacceptable conditions and torture had come to light. However, the treaty was not strictly an exchange, like a prisoner for a prisoner. The first exchange was on December 10, 1977.

Peering out from the darkness, I longed to see the light!

The people who walk in darkness will see a great light. For those who live in a land of deep darkness, a light will shine on them.

Isaiah 9:2

CHAPTER THREE

BACK TO THE U.S.A.

Tijuana, Mexico, October 1981

Leaving Santa Martha was an overwhelming relief. They took us to a small airport on the outskirts of Mexico City. It was late afternoon by the time the plane took off. The airplane was a small Cessna type with about twenty seats. We were not alone; some male inmates were on the plane with us. They seemed as relieved as we were about going on to the prisoner exchange.

The men's prisons could be much crueler than the women's, and the correctional officers thought nothing of punishing anyone who got out of line. So I was sure they were as thankful for the exchange as we were.

The first stop was Hermosillo. They took us to a small house, and the first person I noticed was a young girl with a bruise on her face, sitting on a chair. She had tears running down her cheeks and looked very frightened.

This young girl was in custody because her brother was caught doing some crime and would not turn himself in. Life was very different in Mexico.

There were no beds at this place; the floor was the only option. I tried to get some sleep, but I heard men screaming in pain every few minutes. Finally, my sister yelled, "Tell them what they want to know!"

It was a wave of horror that they could do whatever they wanted, and you had better pray you could make it through.

The following day we left Hermosillo. After boarding the plane, we asked the male inmates what was going on with the guys that were screaming. They said, "They were putting their feet in a bucket of water and putting cattle prods on their private parts!"

When we finally arrived in Tijuana, the Tijuana prison, to be exact, there was more craziness. They had two lines of officers lined up across from each other, and they all had something like a billy club, a long round stick some law enforcement agencies may use to keep everyone in line.

The officers had a young man walk between the two lines, and they all were beating him with the billy clubs as he tried to move between the rows. I would never know why we had to watch it; maybe they did not have any officers to process us in, as they were all in the lineup.

The young man being beaten was a child molester, and that was how they did things at the Tijuana prison. The women's side of the prison was a small area with a row of units with bunk beds. The cells were pretty small, about eight women to a cell, and the children could come and stay with their mothers for a time.

I did not question why a child would be in prison with the mother. After all, it was Mexico. If there were any children present, they would sleep with their mothers.

The place was a madhouse. Women had their children with them, and some of the male prisoners were allowed to come over to the women's side at night. Now *that* was something else!

A familiar wave of sickness washed over me as I heard a woman prisoner in the bunk right across from me moaning. The guy she was with was burning her with a cigarette. I guessed he thought it was funny. Sick!

Suddenly, our cell door burst open, and the correctional officers ordered all of us on the women's side of the prison out of bed and into the night skies. Then they kicked the men out of the area and took all the bedding off the beds, looking for contraband!

I had no idea if they found anything; I was just glad they sent that male inmate back to the other side. During the day, we could all mingle in a common area of the prison, and everyone had a story. We met an American guy who was going on the prisoner exchange. He was a pilot and flew drugs back and forth across the border in a small aircraft until he got caught on the Mexican side.

The cast of characters went on and on, and I believed we all had made bad choices. I pray some of the people I met during my time in prison in Mexico have turned their lives around.

The stark difference in culture and corruption opened my eyes to things I had never dreamed of, and I was sure that sin was everywhere, but it was so blatant in Mexico. It was an education that opened my eyes to so many things. First of all, there could be no more blame games. True victory comes when you look around and realize you have a choice. Do not follow anyone without understanding where it could lead. You may feel like you will live forever when you are young, and no one can stop you. That is great if you are on the right path, but if not, it could be tragic!

The day finally came to leave Mexico, and I told my sister I would kiss the ground when we got back to the U.S.A., and I did!

They took us to San Diego Metropolitan Correctional Center, the federal prison overlooking the bay.

Shortly after arriving, we went before a panel of people, and the team reviewed our situation. Then a man asked me if I knew what I had been.

I said, "No?"

He said, "Sylvia, you have been a flake, so irresponsible!" No one had ever said that to me before, and it was like ice water in the face, a real wake-up call! Now was the time to change everything in my life!

Ephesians 2:1-5 reads:

¹And you hath he quickened, who were dead in trespasses and sins; ²Wherein in times past walked according to the course of this world, according to the prince of the power of the air, the spirit that now works in the children of disobedience: ³Among whom also we all had our conversation in times past in the lust of our flesh and the mind. We were by nature the children of wrath, even as others. ⁴But God, who is rich in mercy, for his great love wherewith he loved us, ⁵Even when we were dead in sin, has quickened us together with Christ.

CHAPTER FOUR

GROWING UP

Seattle, Washington
1953-1969

White Center, known by most as "Rat City," was where I grew up. Rat City was a suburb to the south of Seattle. In many ways, growing up there helped prepare me for the world and all the challenges in my future. But unfortunately, it also more than likely contributed to so many of my wrong choices. I knew life was unfair, and bad things happened to good people, even little children. Some of my girlfriends had people in their families who needed deliverance.

Evil was lurking, waiting for an opportunity to lead any or all of us down the road of deception. The uncanny thing about it was you didn't know you were trapped! Unfortunately, we think it is just how life is, and we can do nothing about it. But I know now that every day, we all have a choice.

I finally learned to seek God when I was in prison. After all, He created me, and He knew the direction I should be going!

Growing up in the projects, I learned to run and hide from anything that made me feel uncomfortable. Sometimes it was good and kept me alive, but other times it kept me from learning and growing up.

I thought that was why drugs were so prevalent; you could escape anything that made you feel uncomfortable. However, you couldn't grow up emotionally if you would not work through the tough stuff.

I was the oldest of eight. My Father, Joe, and my mother, Carolyn, married very young and had eight children in ten years.

My father was a shipyard worker by day and a musician by night. He played guitar, sang, and wrote songs. In 1966, my dad went to L.A., and his agent released his song "Two Tear Drops." It was a beautiful song, but the song "96 Tears" came out simultaneously, and Dad's "Two Tear Drops" was drowned out by "96 Tears."

My Father did not like it when the people trying to help him get his music on the air wanted to change something in his songs, and he would not go for that. He was traumatized when his mother passed away, and I remembered him sobbing and making a vow never to love again because it hurt so much when loved ones died. He kept his emotions hidden, so music was how he expressed himself.

I wished I had his music, but the woman, my Father, was living with when he died said she would burn his written (on paper) music and cassettes if we tried to get it from her. They were not married, so I was sure she did not have a legal right to my Father's music, and since he did not have a will, who did?

I was thinking about two young people getting married and having so many children when they were children themselves; it was crazy! Mother was seventeen, and my Father was nineteen, and I was sure they were overwhelmed most of the time. My father left my mother for another woman when I was a teen, and my mother did not take it well.

You can imagine being left with eight kids when you are twenty-nine years old. As the saying goes, "You made your bed, now sleep in it." She did not get any help from her parents. Rejection could make you do unusual things, and it was touch and go for Mother for a time. I was sure she went into shock, and it took some time for her to come out of it and go to work.

I was the babysitter, housekeeper, and cook. But this was nothing new; I had been doing it off and on since I was about eight years old. I had no idea it was not how it should have been; it was just how it was.

Later, my Father and his new wife, Anita (who had five children when they married), soon had my sister, Rachael.

My Father's family was quite large. His mother had five children when she met my grandfather. After that, they had eight children of their own, and a few years after the youngest was born, they finally were able to get a three-bedroom house. It was small, but it was their home.

My grandfather was from Chile and came to America when he was thirteen. He said some men threw him on a ship, and he never really talked about his family in Chile other than to say he had a crazy uncle. And as far as I knew, he never kept in contact with them. My father's grandmother was Navajo and married a Spanish man; that relationship did not work out, so life was very rough for her and her children.

My mother only had one half-sister. She longed for a large family, and she got it. The family members on both sides thought my parents should have stopped at five children, but my mother disagreed.

Mom did have one more daughter, Stacy. I had already married at sixteen and had my son, Monty. Stacy was born two months after my son. So by this time, I had three whole sisters, two half-sisters, four step sisters, four whole brothers, and one stepbrother. So to say I was comfortable in a crowd is an understatement!

My brother, Tony, was the one who could make us laugh. We would all line up on the couch when our parents were gone, and Tony would play Jerry Lewis. We loved each other, and I guessed we knew this was all we had, and we were thankful for each other. But unfortunately, Tony was full of energy, which got him into trouble. Tony was the oldest of the boys, and Dad would often discipline him in fierce ways.

Even though my family was large, we were comfortable venturing out independently. We did not need someone with us. But of course, we had each other, and all went our separate ways, even as small children. I knew because I was responsible for looking out for my brothers and sisters as the oldest.

We lived in a cul-de-sac with many good-sized families in our neighborhood. The Seffner family was right next to us, and they had nine children. The Kennedys were next to them, and they had five.

Sometimes, I walked to our local lake (named Hicks Lake back then) as I loved to swim. I was about ten at the time, and one day while swimming, an old pickup truck pulled into the parking lot. The man inside the old truck just sat there watching me on the dock.

I started feeling a bit uneasy about this person, so I jumped into the water and got under the dock; there was an air pocket so I could breathe. Finally, I heard the old truck start and leave, so I came out from under the dock. Soon, I felt it was time to head home; I saw a teenage boy leaving the park and asked him if I could walk with him.

When I was about halfway home, the boy told me he had reached his turn off, so we parted ways.

As I was crossing the school field, the same old pickup pulled up, and a short, stalky Hispanic man got out, picked up a broken beer bottle, and started walking towards me. Terror was flooding through me as I saw his glassy eyes and the sweat pouring from his forehead.

I was right near the gym and heard kids in there playing basketball. I pounded on the door, hoping someone would let me in. No luck, so I jumped off the porch into some bushes. Around the corner, the boys in the gym had gone outside. I was so thankful to see them!

The crazy guy must have seen them also and took off. I never said anything about the event, and maybe I thought my parents might not let me go to the lake anymore if I had told them? I was so thankful to God for protecting me and giving me the strength to do what I needed to do in each situation.

One weekend, when I was about fifteen, I was invited to a party in the north end of town. The Seffner family moved up to Lake City, and our mother took us to visit them; the party was at their neighbor's place. As the night went on, things got crazy. Tom Music was a severe drug addict. He was going for a drive and wanted people to go with him.

Tom came up to me and said, "You are coming with me."

I said, "No, I am not going with you!" That was the right choice; he called a few hours later from the King County jail, booked in on murder charges.

I felt so bad for the two guys who did go with him. They were afraid of him, and because they did not want Tom to shoot them, they went with him and got five years for that choice.

I genuinely believed God gave me the courage to stand up to Tom that day.

I could tell of many events and examples when I was young, but I believe you get the picture. I was a mess and so thankful I lived and eventually learned from my bad choices.

My heart's cry is that this book might help others going through tough stuff so they see that God can take the foolish things to confound the wise!

1 Corinthians 1:26-27 reads:

26) *Brothers, consider the time of your calling: not many were wise by human standards; not many were influential; not many were of noble birth.*

27) *But God chose the foolish things of the world to shame the wise; God chose the weak things to shame the strong. So God will take the foolish things to confound the wise!*

CHAPTER FIVE

A NEW PERSPECTIVE

Seattle, Washington, March 1996

It was another rainy day in Seattle as I prepared to meet with Gayle.

We planned to have lunch together, as it had been several years since we had seen each other and expected to catch up.

She was still working for Joe Lacey at Lacey Omalley Bail Bonds and was doing very well. So, we made a plan to meet up for lunch. I was happy to reconnect with her; she was always thoughtful and kind. However, a few hours before we met for lunch, the phone rang, and it was Gayle. She was distraught, and she told me that Joe did not show up for work, and she had gone to check on him, as he was up in years, and he was dead.

She had started working for Joe and Fran Lacey when I had first met her at Christian Faith Center in 1986. Joe and Fran needed help with the business since they had some problems that set them back financially. They trusted Gayle since she had done some work for the company in eastern Washington and had moved to Seattle to help them. Unfortunately, Fran had passed away a few years after Gayle had started working with them in Seattle.

Now, Joe and Fran were both gone, Fran passed away in the early nineties, and Joe had left the company to Gayle. Joe would have left it to his family, but none wanted to work the business. If you didn't work for the company and learn the industry, especially bail bonds, you would not stay in business for very long.

The crafty ones would work you over, and you would have more bills than money. You needed to be a certain kind of person to own a bail bonds business and survive: compassionate, strong, and intelligent. Gayle was all of that.

She asked me if I would work for her, and I agreed that I would for three years. That was more than twenty years ago. When Gayle asked me, a flood of emotions engulfed me. Yet, I knew Gayle needed my help, and I felt God wanted me to do it as well. So, after giving a two-week notice at my current job, I began working for Gayle.

Looking back at all the twists and turns in my life, I could hardly believe I was going to work in such a disheartening industry; then again, I could now speak hope into many others' lives, encouraging them not to give up on that loved one who could not seem to make the right choice. I certainly knew about that.

It took a few weeks before I felt comfortable writing bonds, but Gayle said, "Do it. Write and fill in the spaces on the bond, then get moving; we need to be on it for our clients!"

The language on the bonds took some time to get used to but was very necessary. So I did. Just like swimming, if you don't jump in the water, you will never learn to swim.

Gayle was fearless. One day, a man about six feet, four inches tall, and maybe 280 pounds came into the office and was very upset about a bond recently written. Gayle was about five feet, three inches tall, and stepped right up to the counter, squaring her shoulders. Gayle said, "We posted the bond, and the defendant was out, so it was too late to get his money back, and he has to live with it."

He left, and you could tell he was not happy. I wondered if I could be that strong and tell it how it was? I have since learned that if you can't, you better find another job in an industry that won't require you to.

At the time, I had no idea how much my learning curve was about to increase. Gayle put me on the 12:00 a.m. to 8:00 a.m. shift, so once again, I was to see another side of life: downtown Seattle after midnight. Most people in their right mind would not be interested in seeing that side of life. Was I in my right mind? Only time would tell.

When nothing was going on in the office, I would go up to the jail and get to know the people who dealt with the same people I was dealing with, and I could learn a lot from the correctional officers at the check-in.

One night, while spending time at check-in, a young man came in, and he was not doing well. He kept saying, "Get them off me! They are all over me."

I had no idea what kind of drug he was on, but the officer assured him he could see nothing and told him he had to leave. It took some time, but finally, he left. Drugs could do a horrible thing to the mind!

Working in the bail bonds industry and sitting in courtrooms many days a week magnified that fact, and I knew I understood what drugs did to many lives. I met so many of the officers, and they were very good at dealing with the night-time roamers—the ones who lived on the streets. But one thing was sure: there was an evil force, and we all needed to check our hearts to make sure it was not living in us!

It seemed to me that unforgiveness and fear could trap you, and taking drugs might numb the pain, but your world was about to get scary.

After returning from the jail late one night, a tall, white male with big hair was wearing a white t-shirt and had blood smudged here and there on it. He seemed dazed as he knocked at the office door, wanting in. I did not want to let him in, but I felt sorry for him; he looked like a big, lost kid, frightened and alone. Since I wanted to pray for him, I let him in. I know you might think that was a crazy idea; why not call the police and let them handle it? But I had no fear of this man, and he did let me pray for him for quite a while. He finally left, and I hope he found his way out of that dark hole and found some peace.

Don't get me wrong. I've had times when my gut said, *"No way!* Walk away from this person." God has warned me so many times; sometimes, I would listen, and other times I wished I had. Deception is when things look good but are filled with shadows and lies.

We all face these things at some point in our lives, but it could be an everyday event in the bail bonds industry, and I tried to stay prayed up. Everything was a learning curve for me.

One incident that happened a few months after I started working for Gayle was a real wake-up call for Gayle and her bounty hunters. She received a call that one of her bounty hunters had taken down one of her skips (someone who missed court and would not make a new court date) at a funeral, right in front of the casket! It was anyone's guess why he could not wait for him to leave the room before jumping on him. Naturally, the family of the deceased was livid, and rightly so. Gayle asked me to visit the family and assure them she would make it right.

At that time, the laws regarding bail bond companies and bounty hunters were unclear. Gayle realized that something needed to change. So she got busy looking into how to do this. Sure enough, she got the ball rolling. Because of Gayle's actions, new regulations were implemented in Washington State. Bounty hunters were required to be licensed and insured and required some law enforcement training. No more of the Wild West!

Eventually, Gayle established an office in Kent, about twenty minutes south of Seattle. So I would have my own office to run, which allowed me to meet the community.

Years earlier, I was trying to get back on my feet after getting out of prison. I was praying about so many things when suddenly, the Holy Spirit moved on my heart and opened my eyes to all that law enforcement went through. I knew most people in prison did not like authority, and their attitude reflected that whenever confronted.

My heart broke for the men and women working in that career, knowing the battle they faced. I honestly didn't know how they did it without the Spirit of God revealing how to handle every situation. I prayed for them often. I would have many occasions to meet those who had chosen to stand in the gap for us and face those captured by the evil one, Satan!

Gayle thought it would be a good idea to start going to the courts. The Regional Justice Center had many different things going on, so many courtrooms to check out and see if anyone needed my help.

I had no idea this was not common; Gayle told me to go, so I did. I would go to court five days a week and believe me, that opened my eyes to so many things.

In the morning, I would go to the ground floor, room A, known as courtroom G.A. is where they would do felony arraignments, and this was where I learned so much about the Revised Code of Washington, also known as the RCW's and how the court operates. One day Gayle wanted me to meet up with John Henry Browne, a high-profile attorney in Seattle.

John had a client who needed my help—a business owner with domestic issues. The judge set his bail at seven hundred and fifty thousand dollars, and 10 percent of that is a non-refundable fee. In addition, the court ordered him to go to a drug and alcohol treatment center as soon as he got out of jail.

As we were leaving the defendant's bank on a Friday afternoon, the defendant stated, "I am on my way to treatment." So imagine my shock on Monday morning when I heard on the news that this defendant's family was being held hostage at gunpoint by him!

I learned that he had the cab driver drop him off and did not go to treatment. Instead, he got more drugs and alcohol, which was a lousy combination that would put you in Stupidville! I went to see him in jail about a week later and asked him what he was thinking? He said, "The gun was not loaded!" His sentence was eleven years.

The court was never dull, and I would always listen to how a judge would rule on a case regarding bail or not. However, when I first started, the court was much more cautious about releasing someone who had a criminal history.

Whenever I met with the defendants' family members, more often than not, they would feel hopeless. I was sure my family felt that way when they had first heard about Pam and me getting caught with drugs.

So my outlook would be compassionate but firm. You could not give up; this was the time to speak up and let your loved ones know it was the time to face the issues. Some seemed to learn by making mistakes, while others were pretty content with seeing others make mistakes and knew that was a bad idea.

In the meantime, Gayle had met a wonderful man named Denny. The first time they met was at a CrimeStoppers meeting in December 2000. He was a U.S. marshal and was very active in CrimeStoppers. Denny was just what she was looking for, a great guy. They married in June of 2002. Denny should write a book; he has some fantastic stories.

Both Denny and Gayle have made the bail bonds industry a better industry by working with the local representatives and getting higher standards regarding education and training put into law.

In this day and age, the opportunity to walk into deception is endless. So many things seem right, yet they lead to total darkness. The most important thing you can do is seek God's wisdom in dealing with loved ones. He created them, and He knows what it will take to lead them out of that darkness.

Ephesians 2:4-5 says, *"But God being rich in mercy, because of the great love with which he loved us, even when we were dead in our trespasses, made us alive together with Christ. Thus, by grace, His amazing grace, we can be saved! Thank God!"*

Proverbs 3:3-4 says, *"Let not mercy and truth forsake you: bind them around your neck; write them in your heart: So you shall find favor and understanding in the sight of God."*

CHAPTER SIX

THE REGIONAL JUSTICE CENTER

In March of 1997, the Regional Justice Center (R.J.C.) opened the south end division of King County Courts (Superior and District), and Gayle opened an office in a small house not too far from the facility. Gayle asked me to run this office.

The jail staff used the house while waiting for the R.J.C. to open, so I met some jail staff, which was a blessing. They would fill me in on the proper way to conduct yourself when posting bonds or to go to the jail to visit inmates.

I had no idea if other counties had two county jails, but finding someone in the first twenty-four hours could be tricky.

When you were looking for someone picked up by the police and taken into custody, it could be confusing for everyone. For example, which jail was the person taken to? King County jail in Seattle or Kent? Depending on the crime and location, they could also be taken to the Kent City jail.

The morning calendar at R.J.C. from 9:00 a.m. to 11:00 a.m. was the felony arraignment calendar. That was where I learned from and worked with so many attorneys, private attorneys, and county-appointed attorneys. I would listen to the attorneys' arguments and the judge's rulings; this was fascinating.

Of course, the families and loved ones of the defendants were traumatized, and it would take time to walk them through the process and let them know the responsibility they were taking on when they took on the liability of bail with a bail bond company.

Most people think you pay ten percent, and that is it; there is a lot more to it than that. If the defendant does not show up, you are responsible for the total bail amount, not just the ten percent. If the defendant is a no- show, you have a certain amount of time to get the defendant to reschedule the court date and show up. Otherwise, you will need to give the bonding company the money to pay the court or provide them with cash to pay the bounty hunter to find them and put them back in jail. So I would meet with the indemnitors (those taking on the liability) and let them know what they were taking on.

There would usually be someone there for the defendant with the morning calendar. The afternoon calendar was another story; a defendant was taken into custody to investigate a possible felony. They would be held for a certain amount of time and charged or released.

On the afternoon investigation calendar, I would possibly need to go to the jail and visit the defendant, and I would ask them if they needed me to call anyone.

One particular case stood out to me: a young man was in for domestic violence, and he did not have anyone who could help him, but because he had his own business and was a homeowner, I could help him.

He came home early one day to find his wife in a compromising position with someone else. He attacked the man, so they arrested him. They had two young children who meant the world to him, and he wanted the marriage to work; unfortunately, she did not feel the same way. The court had put a no-contact order in place, and he was worried sick about his children.

One day, he was at the mall and saw his wife and kids with this man. He said the man had said something about his young daughter, and he flipped out and attacked the man again. So he went back to jail, and he would not be getting out this time.

He lost everything during his time in jail, and when he finally got out, it was time to start over. In the meantime, we had had a string of bank robberies they called the River Bandit, as they believed that was the getaway mode. However, the bandit did make a mistake one day, and a Kent police officer found one small fingerprint. You guessed it; it was him! He called me, and I went to visit him in jail. He felt he had nothing to lose and would do his time, and one day after doing his time, he would leave this county.

Another time when I was at the afternoon investigation calendar, I saw them bring in two people from Scotland. They had been arrested at the airport because they were trying to bring in some form of marijuana. I knew I had to visit them and see if I could help in any way. They said they did not have anyone I could call and were shocked when I told them they would not be going anywhere anytime soon.

I felt so bad for them; at least when I was in Mexico, I had someone to call! I talked with an attorney I knew one day and mentioned the situation to him about the couple. It turned out he was Scottish and said he wanted to help them. It took several months, working out a deal with the prosecuting attorney, and getting the case closed. It would have taken much longer if Mr. Danko had not stepped in. I was thankful for the many attorneys that I had the privilege to work with and help make the process easier for their clients.

Most of them, private or appointed, worked tirelessly, and I was sure they had many days where they wondered if they had made the right career choice.

I have prayed for all in the arena of the R.J.C., from maintenance to judges and everyone in between. I realized we were all people with struggles and needed wisdom every day.

The struggles are real, and I believe we will find answers if we seek the Truth. God Almighty created us for unique things, and if we take a few minutes every day and thank Him, even if it is only for an opportunity to take another breath and ask Him how we become all that He created us to be, He will guide us, if we seek Him.

I know without a doubt God has created us for good things. Having a relationship with Jesus is the starting of great wisdom. Christians are called to be a blessing and reflect His goodness. We are to be a part of the answer and have a heart filled with peace, even in the darkest of times. We all should know that the struggle is between good and evil, and we all must choose who we will serve.

With everything going on in the world right now, we must ask hard questions about the motivation of our hearts; Truth does matter in our lives. Are we being deceived on any level?

When I would visit a defendant in jail, I often tried to get them to look at their choices and stop blaming someone else. For example, I would remind them that they chose their partner and must own up to their part of the situation in domestic violence cases.

If the person repeatedly ended up in jail for domestic violence, I would tell them to repent and ask Jesus to help them before the Evil One dragged them into the pit of Hell. If they ended up there, they would recall those who tried to tell them Hell is real. God did not create Hell for them; He made it for the fallen angels and the demons.

I did not want anyone's blood on my hands. If the Holy Spirit told me to warn someone, I would warn them. I learned that at a young age at a wake for a friend of mine. She had six sons and one daughter. One of the boys had a hard time with his mother's death. The Holy Spirit wanted me to speak with him, but someone was talking to me about something, and I thought, *Yes, as soon as they finished the conversation.*

I could see him driving away on his motorcycle when I went to look for him, and we did not have cell phones at that time. I was staying in their family home at the time, and at about 3:00 a.m., I heard a knock at the door. An officer was there with a helmet in his hand. The son I was supposed to speak with would not be coming home; he died in a motorcycle crash!

Despair gripped my soul, but I learned a lesson about the timing of the Lord; when He gives me an impression to speak with someone, I do.

It was like writing this book—I have no idea if it will mean anything to anyone, but I must obey the Lord. He says, "Write," so I write and pray it will help someone somewhere.

So the scripture I have for this chapter is John 3:16: *"God so loved the world that he gave his one and only son, that whoever believes in him shall not perish but have eternal life"*

(King James Version).

CHAPTER SEVEN

THE REASON

Israel, November 1995

In 1995, I went to Israel with Matthew and Carol Swartz. They had put together a prayer team from many different churches. Joe and Linda Knight, pastors of the Rock Church, were my pastors and had invited Matthew and Carol to our church, knowing the mission. I was thankful to be going and to see where Jesus had walked!

When we arrived in Israel, the country was in mourning. Yitzhak Rabin had been assassinated a few weeks before we arrived, and it was a hectic time coming through the airport.

Matthew had put the team together to pray while Matthew and Carol met with Benjamin Netanyahu, a political figure at the Knesset. Benjamin was running for the office of Prime Minister in the upcoming elections. Everyone who joined them loved to pray!

The Lord instructed him to encourage Benjamin and tell him he would be the next prime minister. Matthew was allowed access to the Knesset and Benjamin because one of his relatives had been in a powerful position in the government of Israel.

Matthew said when Benjamin heard it, he laughed and thought it was doubtful, as his numbers were so low in the polls after the assassination of Yitzak Rabin. However, Matthew reassured Benjamin that God had his back.

It was amazing how small Israel was, yet there was a mighty spirit in its people to protect and defend all who came to live in peace. Both males and females would enlist in the Israeli defense forces at eighteen years old.

One evening while we were in Jerusalem, praying over the city, Matthew came up to me and told me I would write a book. I thought, *What are you saying? Me? What could I possibly have to say?*

A book? In my mind, I had nothing of value to share, and yet, I knew my Lord and Savior had protected me so many times. I knew I did not deserve it. He had mercy on me!

After becoming a bail bondswoman, the Spirit of the living God revealed so many things to me as I watched our legal system play out the good, the bad, and the ugly.

I had to face the fact that the road to Hell seemed to be paved with good intentions. But unfortunately, we seem to make excuses for ourselves and our loved ones when we act on that negative impulse. We all need wisdom to not fall into the trap of deception.

Now, I know many of you may not believe in Heaven and Hell, but might I inject one critical thought? If Hell is real, are you willing to place your whole eternity on your belief? Because if you are wrong, you will have an eternity to think about it. Know that when you read this, my heart cried out for you to understand how much God loves you! If I am wrong, I lived a life believing in peace and love and trying to be someone to give those in distress hope.

My heart's cry is for everyone who hungers to know what is going on and how to have peace that passes all understanding in these troubled times. If you would just call out and ask God to show you the **Truth**, not according to us and our ways, but according to the Creator of Heaven and Earth. God longs for a relationship with us!

God has given us the freedom to choose: forgive or not forgive? Think about it. Who is the prisoner in that situation? Peace or fear, love or hate, confusion or a sound mind?

The heart of the matter is within us; are our motives selfish? Is pride found in us? Pride was found in Satan, and he was banished from heaven. Any gift or talent we have, God created us and gave it to us, and we are to be thankful, not prideful.

The one who created you gave you every gift and ability. Granted, not everyone uses the skills given to them, but God gave them to us!

What we do with them is our choice. Use your gifts or let them go to waste. The gifts were given to be a blessing to others. That is the heart of God. I know for sure I do not want to gain the whole world and lose my soul!

I pray that the one who died for you and me, who loved us enough to lay it all down and take on our sin, becomes real to you. King Jesus will be on the throne in the end. His goodness will overcome evil. Everyone who will choose to know, love, and develop a relationship with Jesus will come to understand His amazing love and win in the future!

Revelation 21: 1-7: King James Version

1) *And I saw a new heaven and a new earth; for the first heaven and the first earth were passed away, and there was no more sea.*

2) *And I John saw the holy city, new Jerusalem, coming down from God out of heaven, prepared as a bride adorned for her husband.*

3) *And I heard a great voice out of heaven saying, behold, the tabernacle of God is with men, and he will dwell with them, and they shall be his people, and God himself shall be with them, and be their people.*

4) *And God shall wipe away all their tears from their eyes; and there shall be no more death, neither sorrow, nor crying, neither shall there be any more pain: for the former things are passed away.*

5) *And he that sat upon the throne said, Behold, I make all things new. And he said to me, Write: for these words are true and faithful.*

6) *And he said unto me; It is done. I am the Alpha and Omega, the beginning and the end. So I will give unto him that is athirst of the fountain of the water of life freely.*

7) *He that overcometh shall inherit all things; and I will be his God, and he shall be my son.*

www.ingramcontent.com/pod-product-compliance
Lightning Source LLC
Chambersburg PA
CBHW052123030426
42335CB00025B/3083